ALL THE PRAISE

52 WEEKS OF
PRAISE DEVOTIONS

ALL THE
PRAISE
52 WEEKS OF
PRAISE DEVOTIONS

Triple J Publishing
Sanford, North Carolina

Ophelia W. Livingston

All The Praise: 52 Weeks of Praise Devotions
Copyright ©2009 by Ophelia W. Livingston

Requests for information should be addressed to:
OWL Risk Management Consulting, LLC

      International Bible Society
      1820 Jet Stream Drive
      Colorado Springs, Colorado 80921, USA
      In the US, phone: (719) 488-9200

Cover Design by Triple J Publishing
Edited by Barbara S. Keller
ISBN: 978-0-9840853-2-3
Religion/Spirituality

Triple J Publishing, Sanford, North Carolina
© 2009 by Triple J Publishing
Printed in the United States of America

For more information go to www.praisediet.com or email at ophelia@praisediet.com

About the Author

Ophelia W. Livingston is a devoted and anointed woman of God who has been involved in church music and church choirs for over 30 years. Currently, she serves as the Minister of Music at First Calvary Missionary Baptist Church in Sanford, North Carolina. Ophelia has authored the following books:

Job Descriptions for Today's Ministry

All The Praise: 52 Weeks of Praise Devotions

A Music Ministry Handbook: For Music Leaders

In addition:

Ophelia's credentials are as follows: Bachelor of Science, Business Administration, University of North Carolina at Greensboro; Master of Business Administration, Information Security, Salem International University; and Master of Science in Information Systems (MSIS) University of Fairfax. Ophelia specializes in assisting small businesses, churches and ministries incorporate, and setup their internal control policies. She has the following certifications: Certified Internal Control Management Professional, Certified Governance, Risk & Compliance Manager. She can be reached by e-mail at ophelia@praisediet.com or toll-free: 1-866-579-7475.

Call today to plan a workshop or seminar.

ACKNOWLEDGEMENTS

I thank God that my relationship with Him not only deepened after writing this book, but has flourished and reached a level that keeps me in awe of His goodness. I have been on the **Praise Diet Plan** that has totally strengthened my belief in Him. He is more than worthy of my praise.

A giant thanks goes out to my wonderful husband James, who continues to stand by my side and is my lion in the midst of all my battles. He is my support and my comforter and for that I am grateful. A special thanks to my three daughters Jamelia, Janel and Jewel. Without them I would not have had the inspiration to write this book.

Last but not least is my dad, Ross, who guided my early years and taught me the true meaning of *"All The Praise"*. Dad, you blessed me with a biblical and a Christian foundation that enabled me to cross many treacherous bridges in my life. Even when I thought I had no hope and could not see my way through, your endless strength and love pushed me to continue on my journey. I love you dearly.

Introduction

The assembled church is to sing to God and edify each other when we come together. *"Let the word of Christ dwell in you richly as you teach and admonish one another with all wisdom, and as you sing psalms, hymns and spiritual songs with gratitude in your hearts to God"* Colossians 3:16; NIV. "Dwell in you richly" actually means to "fill the house with riches." This scripture speaks of our being filled with the riches of God's Word, out of which will come true worship. The Bible tells us to sing with understanding. If you cannot hear the words then you certainly cannot worship with understanding.

Paul gives the same instruction to the church at Ephesus where he connects the singing and the singer to being filled with the Spirit. *"Do not get drunk on wine, which leads to debauchery. Instead, be filled with the Spirit. [19]Speak to one another with psalms, hymns and spiritual songs. Sing and make music in your heart to the Lord, [20]always giving thanks to God the Father for everything, in the name of our Lord Jesus Christ"* Ephesians. 5:18-20; NIV.

God sets a high standard for music in the church. It should never simply be "music for music's sake." The music we play and sing must come from the riches of God's Word and in the fullness of His Spirit in us. When music is used under the influence of the Holy Spirit, it prepares the way for the preacher to preach. We do not "work up" worship by the music, but rather, true music comes from a worshipful heart.

Church musicians are not performers or entertainers that attract attention to themselves, but lead the congregation to God. If we leave the service drawn to the singer or singers, then something went wrong. Music must be **God-centered and not man-centered**, which is operating in the flesh. We do not use God to display man's talents, but man's talents are used to display God. Any offering that is not acceptable to God will not bring spiritual or eternal benefits to God's people, no matter how much they enjoy what they hear or do. If the beat or music supersedes the message, then we are not leading people to God through the scriptures and have merely performed meaningless entertainment.

True worship was never intended to "get them in," but rather, to be an expression of church members' worship because "they are in."

Why You Should Praise God

God makes a very powerful promise in 1 Corinthians 10:13.

> *"No temptation has overtaken you except such as is common to man; but God is faithful, who will not allow you to be tempted beyond what you are able, but with the temptation will also make the way of escape, that you may be able to bear it."*

- Praising God lets you draw near to God.
- Praising God makes you less fearless of the things in the world.
- Praising God means you believe in God's promises.
- Praising God allows you to stand up against your enemies. The enemies cannot stand to hear you praise God out loud.
- Praising God will transform your life.

When you praise God, you:
1. Focus on His proven character and His faithfulness to His promises.
2. Demonstrate that you put more trust in God's promises than in your problems. This is what I call faith. And I know that the God I serve responds to faith.

Seven Ways to Praise

Praise!

There are many dimensions of praise. In many ways, praise is a very important aspect of our relationship with God. At all times God inhabits our praise and we should not be inhibited in our praise, for our praise glorifies God.

As you begin your spiritual "Praise Diet" plan for praise, it is important to get an understanding of the seven different dimensions of praising God. In the Hebrew language there are seven words that are synonymous with the English word praise.

As you read and study these seven dimensions of praise, the format of study is as follows; you are given the word, then its meaning and finally biblical verses to study and reflect on.

Towdah

Yadah

Barak

Shabach

Zamar

Halal

Tehillah

Towah

Towah (Todah) is the sacrifice of praise. Specially, Towah is literally extending your hand in adoration. Towah is praising the Lord in spite of the fact that things are upside down in your own world. Towah is praising the Lord, even if you do not feel like praising Him. You will praise the Lord even though you are going through many trials in your life. This is your sacrifice to God.

Hebrews 13:15
By Him therefore let us offer the sacrifice of praise to God continually, that is, the fruit of our lips giving thanks to His name.

Jeremiah 33:11
The voice of joy, and the voice of gladness, the voice of the bridegroom, and the voice of the bride, the voice of them that shall say, Praise the Lord of hosts: for the Lord is good; for his mercy endureth forever: and of them that shall bring the sacrifice of praise into the house of the Lord.

Psalms 54:6
I will freely sacrifice unto thee: I will praise thy name, O Lord; for it is good.

Yadah

Yadah is the demonstration of our love and submission to the Lord by the raising of our hands or to throw out the hand. Yadah is lifting your hands to the Lord in total submission and devotion. Yadah places you in the dimension of where you begin to take control over your mind and body.

Lamentations 3:41
Let us lift up our heart with our hands unto God in the Heavens.

Psalms 134:2
Lift up your hands in the sanctuary, and bless the Lord.

Psalms 63:4
Thus will I bless thee while I live: I will lift up my hands in thy name.

2 Chronicles 20:21
And when he had consulted with the people, he appointed singers unto the LORD, and that should praise the beauty of holiness, as they went out before the army, and to say, Praise the LORD; for his mercy endureth for ever.

Barak

Barak means to bow. It has a primitive root meaning "to kneel". Barak is to be completely overwhelmed by His majesty and bow at His feet in submission and honor to the Lord. Barak is witnessed when the Holy Spirit begins to manifest during worship.

Ephesians 3:13 & 14
Wherefore I desire that ye faint not at my tribulations for you, which is your glory. [14]For this cause I bow my knees unto the Father of our Lord Jesus Christ.

Romans 14:11
For it is written, As I live, saith the Lord, every knee shall bow to me, and every tongue shall confess to God.

Psalms 95:6
O come, let us worship and bow down: let us kneel before the Lord our maker.

Shabach

Shabach means to shout. Shabach is giving praise to the Lord in the form of a shout. When you are in the midst of Shabach you are lifting your voice unto the Lord, giving praise for what He has done and what He is going to do.

Psalms 98:7
Let the sea roar, and the fullness thereof; the world, and they that dwell there

Ezra 3:11
And they sang together by course in praising and giving thanks unto the LORD; because He is good, for His mercy endureth for ever toward Israel. And all the people shouted with a great shout, when they praised the LORD, because the foundation of the house of the LORD was laid.

Isaiah 12:6
Cry out and shout, thou inhabitant of Zion: for great is the Holy One of Israel in the midst of thee.

Zamar

Zamar means to play any instrument that glorifies the Lord. Zamar is not the first thing you do when you praise God. The first thing you do is to extend your praise with Yadah and Towdah.

Psalms 150

Praise Ye the Lord. Praise God in His sanctuary: praise Him in the firmament of His power. [2]Praise Him for His mighty acts: praise Him according to His excellent greatness. [3]Praise Him with the sound of the trumpet: praise Him with the psaltery and harp. [4]Praise Him with the timbrel and dance: praise Him with stringed instruments and organs. [5]Praise Him upon the loud cymbals: praise Him upon the high-sounding cymbals. [6]Let everything that hath breath praise the Lord. Praise Ye the Lord.

Halal

Halal means to rave and boast of the wonders of the Lord with great excitement through dance. Praise is found in the Old Testament more than 160 times. The word Hallelujah, comes from the root word Halal meaning "to shine", "to make a show" or "to rave".

2 Chronicles 23:13
And she looked, and, behold, the king stood at his pillar at the entering in, and the princes and the trumpets by the king: and all the people of the land rejoiced, and sounded with trumpets, also the singers with instruments of music, and such as taught to sing praise.

Psalms 149:3
Let them praise His name in the dance: let them sing praises unto Him with the timbrel and harp.

II Samuel 6:16
And as the Ark of the Lord came into the city of David, Michal Saul's daughter looked through a window, and saw king David leaping and dancing before the Lord.

Psalms 30:11
Thou hast turned for me my mourning into dancing: thou hast put off my sackcloth, and girded me with gladness.

Tehillah

Tehillah means combining singing, shouting, dancing, clapping and rejoicing as you show praise before the Lord.

Psalms 47:1
O clap your hands, all ye people: shout unto God with the voice of triumph.

Psalms 47:6
Sing praises to God, sing praises; sing praises unto our King, sing praises.

Psalms 144:9
I will sing a new song unto thee, O God:
upon a psaltery and an instrument of ten strings will I sing praises unto thee.

Ephesians 5:19-20

Speaking to yourselves in psalms and hymns and spiritual song; singing and making melody in your heart to the Lord. [20] Giving thanks always for all things unto God and the Father in the name of our Lord Jesus Christ.

What Can Praise Do?

Praise is essential to the knowledge of God and His will. The strength of your life is the strength of the song in your heart. When the pressure of life is heavy, that is the time to sing a song of praise. Pressure is permitted to strengthen the attitude and spirit of praise. There are hundreds of reasons you can use to praise God. Listed below are twelve reasons praise affects your walk with God.

1. Praise, helps you honor God

2. Praise, undergirds your faith

3. Praise, brings you deliverance

4. Praise, is a voice of your faith

5. Praise, is the language the angels in Heaven sing

6. Praise, sets the stage for God to move in your life

7. Praise, fuels joy, which is your strength

8. Praise, knocks down the wall of resistance

9. Praise, is always in front of your blessings

10. Praise, brings the presence of God on the scene

11. Praise, is the highway faith uses to move its blessings, and

12. Praise, gives God the right to help you.

Get Up and Put On Your Praise

*"No time should be lost in returning thanks to the Lord for His mercies; for our praises are most acceptable, pleasant and profitable, when they flow from a full heart. By this, love and gratitude would be more excited and more deeply fixed in the hearts of believers; the events would be more known and longer remembered. Whatever Deborah, Barak, or the army had done, the Lord must have **All The Praise**. The will, the power, and the success were all from Him." Judges 5:6-11. Matthew Henry's Concise Commentary*

Praise Is...

Week 1 - 1 Samuel 17:37

Praise Is Acknowledging God For What He Has Done, For What He Is Doing And For What He Will Do

"David said moreover, The LORD that delivered me out of the paw of the lion, and out of the paw of the bear, he will deliver me out of the hand of this Philistine. And Saul said unto David, Go, and the LORD be with thee."

May today, you find peace within. May you trust that you are exactly where you are meant to be. May you not forget the infinite possibilities that are born of faith in yourself and in people around you. May you use the gifts that you have received, and pass on the love that has been given to you. May you be content with yourself, just the way you are. Let this knowledge settle into your bones, and allow your soul the freedom to sing, dance, praise, shout and love. God's love is there for each and every one of us.

Musical Selections:

Gospel: Be Glorified

Hymn: O For A Thousand Tongues

Prayer:

Father I stretch my hands to thee, no other help I know. Amen.

Week 2 – 1 Chronicles 16:34

Praise Is About An Attitude Of Thankfulness

"O give thanks unto the LORD; for He is good; for His mercy endureth for ever."

Let God be glorified in our praises. Let others be edified and taught, that strangers to Him may be led to adore Him. Let ourselves triumph and trust in God. Those that give glory to God's name are allowed to glorify in it. Let the everlasting covenant be the great matter of our joy.

Show forth from day to day His salvation, His promised salvation by Christ. We have reason to celebrate from day to day; for we daily receive the Christ's benefit, and it is a subject that can never be exhausted. In the midst of our praises, we must not forget to pray for the humble servants of God in distress.

Musical Selections:

> **Gospel:** O Give Thanks Unto the Lord

> **Hymn:** Glory To His Name

Prayer:

Thank you for blessing me yet another day. Amen.

Week 3 – II Chronicles 20:21

Praise Is All About Your Faith. Use Your Voice To Sing His Praise

"*And when he had consulted with the people, he appointed singers unto the LORD, and that should praise the beauty of holiness, as they went out before the army, and to say, Praise the LORD; for his mercy endureth for ever.*"

Have you ever wondered why bad things happen to good people? I know I have, I have even asked God the question, "Why did you take the time to dump on me today?" God answered me, proclaiming, "It is all about your faith." God said you have to trust me. You have to believe and have faith that I will take care of you. I am your Father, in me there is no other. I will love and protect you. I will challenge you with trials and tribulations. These things I do unto to you so that you will become stronger in your faith. When you overcome the challenges that I have given you, you will become a better person. Only when you let go and let God, will you find your voice to sing praises unto me.

Musical Selections:

> **Gospel:** Praise Is What I Do
>
> **Hymn:** My Faith Looks Up To Thee

Prayer:

Lord, help me not to be so caught up in the technicalities that I miss the heart of the person. Amen.

Week 4 – Psalms 7:17

Praise Is About Being On One Accord With God

"I will praise the LORD according to His righteousness: and will sing praise to the name of the LORD most high."

After you let Jesus enter into your heart, you wanted to share the news with everyone. You wanted to fellowship with other believers. You began praising God, proclaiming how good He is and what He has done for you in your life. Fellowship in "one accord" never includes the unbeliever, but those who believe and trust in Him. God has called us out of darkness and placed us in His glorious light. He commands all believers to go out to the world and preach His gospel to all who will hear. Praise God, because He has been good to you and your loved ones this week.

Musical Selections:

> **Gospel:** Get On One Accord, Lift Jesus

> **Hymn:** He's Still Working On Me

Prayer:

Holy Father, I surrender my life to you in all things. My trust is in you and my hope is in you. Have your way in my life and do your will. Allow me to serve your purpose with a willing attitude of humility. Mend my troubled heart and allow my cup to overflow with joy. Amen.

Week 5 – Psalms 40:3

Praise Is Mightier Than My Mountain

"And He hath put a new song in my mouth, even praise unto our God: many shall see it, and fear, and shall trust in the Lord."

Lift up your hands and say: The Lord is equipping and empowering me to do His work in healing, deliverance and empowerment. I will rise to the challenge and obey His every commandment. I will help those around me and comfort then. I will praise Him today, for the Holy Father has showered me with His blessings. I will shout His praises from the mountaintops to all that will hear His word.

Musical Selections:

> **Gospel:** I Can Make This Journey

> **Hymn:** A Mighty Fortress Is Our God

Prayer:

Father, we want to be your gateway, where the angels of God are ascending and descending upon this temple. We want to be the carrier of your glory and spread your glory throughout the earth. We pray for a clear path to heaven to guide the meeting of believers so that we can touch you, know you, and experience you in a wider, deeper, higher, closer way in Jesus' name. Amen

Week 6 – Acts 16:25

Praise Is A Middle Of The Night Shout

"And at midnight Paul and Silas prayed, and sang praises unto God: and the prisoners heard them."

"Shake, shake, shake! Shake the devil off." Have you ever had to get up out of your bed at night and give God some praise? I have, many times. This is what I call it "MY MIDNIGHT PRAISE". I remember jumping out of my bed and running down the hall to get my shout and praise on. I praised Him for taking care of my family. I praised Him for taking care of me. I praised Him for releasing the devil's grip from my loved ones and friends. This is my midnight shout, my midnight praise, my midnight Hallelujah, my midnight moment to tell God how much I really need Him and His love.

Musical Selections:

> **Gospel:** Shout Now, Don't Wait 'Till the Battle Is Over
>
> **Hymn:** Shout to the Lord

Prayer:

Bring to remembrance, that even though I am now wearing these adult shoes, I am still your child in need of training and molding. Amen.

Week 7 – Revelation 12:11

Praise Is My Personal Testimony That I Passed His Test

"And they overcame him by the blood of the Lamb, and by the word of their testimony; and they loved not their lives unto the death."

God has given us four keys to find strength through adversity:

1) Get up in the inside - Maintain an attitude of faith and confidence that we will overcome the problem or situation with the help of God;

2) Trust God's timing - Be patient and understand that God has an appointed time to answer our prayers and bring our desires to pass;

3) Cooperate with God in the midst of adversity - Be willing to change and become the person God wants us to be, and

4) Allow God to use adversity to push us into our divine destiny - be acceptable to God's divine will.

Musical Selections:

      Gospel: I've Got a Testimony

      Hymn: Blessed Assurance

Prayer:

Praise the name of Jesus for He is my rock and He is my deliverer. Praise God for He is my fortress and in Him will I trust. Amen.

Week 8 – Nehemiah 9:5

Praise Is My Forever

"Stand up and bless the LORD your God forever and ever: and blessed be thy glorious name which is exalted above all blessings and PRAISE."

The Lord is equipping and empowering me to do His work. Praise Ye The Lord. I will praise God because of who He is and what He has done in my life.

Musical Selections:

Gospel: Stand By Me

Hymn: Stand Up, Stand for Jesus

Prayer:

Lord Jesus, I believe you are the Son of God. Thank you for dying on the cross for my sins. Please forgive my sins and give me the gift of eternal life. I ask you into my life and heart to be my Lord and Savior. I want to serve you always. Amen.

Week 9 – Isaiah 54:17

Praise Is A Supernatural Weapon For Spiritual Warfare

"No weapon that is formed against thee shall prosper; and every tongue that shall rise against thee in judgment thou shalt condemn. This is the heritage of the servants of the LORD, and their righteousness is of me, saith the LORD."

Jesus told Paul, my strength is your praise. God's power is made perfect in your weakness. Rejoice, when you are weak. Rejoice when you go through trials. Praise God because as a believer, you will see His power break through.

Musical Selections:

    Gospel: No Weapon

    Hymn: A Mighty Fortress Is Our God

Prayer:

Almighty God, the eternal and unshakable fortress where we can find our strength, we praise you for gaining our victory through Jesus Christ. We thank you for giving us hope through Christ's work of salvation through the cross, sustaining us when we are faced with difficult and challenging circumstances. Amen.

Week 10 – Isaiah 22:24

Praise Is Having All The Glory

"And they shall hang upon him all the glory of his father's house, the offspring and the issue, all vessels of small quantity, from the vessels of cups, even to all the vessels of flagons."

Do you know that you are a descendent of royalty? All of the glory of your Father's house is worth praising. You are a descendent of David and you have the authority of David. As Eliakim was of royal blood, you will be of royal blood. God will place the Key of David on your shoulder which is a place of high honor for your family. Jesus has extended His love to all of you.

Musical Selections:

Gospel: All the Glory

Hymn: Glory, Glory Hallelujah

Prayer:

Glory be to the Father, and to the Son, and to the Holy Spirit. As it was in the beginning, is now, and ever shall be, world without end. Amen.

Week 11 – Psalms 22:3

Praise Is Being Thankful

"But thou art holy, O thou that inhabitest the praises of Israel."

God "dwells" in the atmosphere of His praise. This means that praise is not merely a reaction from coming into His presence. Praise is a vehicle of faith which brings us into the presence and power of God. "Praise and worship" is the "gate-pass" which allows us to enter the sacredness of His glory. The psalmist writes, "Enter into His gates with thanksgiving, and into His courts with praise: be thankful unto him, and bless his name" (Psalms 100:4).

There are many actions involved with praise to God — verbal expressions of adoration and thanksgiving, singing, playing instruments, shouting, dancing, lifting or clapping our hands.

Musical Selections:

> **Gospel:** Encourage Yourself
>
> **Hymn:** Lift Your Heads

Prayer:

Teach me the difference between judgment and discernment and to cover my mouth so that I may not gossip about either. Amen.

Week 12 – Psalms 34:1

Praise Is Blessing the Lord At All Times

"I will bless the Lord at all times; His praise shall continually be in my mouth."

To bless God is to recognize the splendor of His richness. He, who is bigger and greater than any other, deserves our praise. A magnifying glass is used to makes objects appear bigger. God is big; He isn't getting any bigger. But He will always be bigger than any of us. You can get an even better perspective of who He is when you magnify Him in your heart.

However, we have a tendency not to magnify God. We magnify our problems, we magnify our enemies, and we magnify our fears. It is time for us to stop and reverse our actions today. Stop magnifying everything except God! He not only wants our praise, but he wants us to magnify Him and all of His greatness.

Musical Selections:

>**Gospel:** God Said He Would Be With Me

>**Hymn:** My Soul Shall Live With Jesus

Prayer:

When I think how far you have brought me, I lack the words to express myself. I give you praise all the time. **YOU** will remain my loving Father forever. Amen.

Week 13 – Psalms 40:3

Praise Is Thanking God For A Brand New Life

"And he hath put a new song in my mouth even praise unto our God: many shall see it, and fear, and shall trust in the Lord."

Have you been born again? If your answer is yes, you are a new creature. Jesus went from dying on the cross to rising on the third day. Yes, He is alive. Give praise to God and to the Son, Jesus Christ. In His great mercy He has given us a new birth, a brand new life with new meaning, and a hope that places our future with Him. We all are alive because Jesus Christ rose from the dead, dying for our sins. He has given us new birth so that we might share what belongs to Him. It is a gift that can never be destroyed. Therefore, I praise God for my brand new life.

Musical Selections:

> **Gospel:** A Brand New Life

> **Hymn:** I Will Trust in the Lord

Prayer:

I will trust the Lord at all times. Amen.

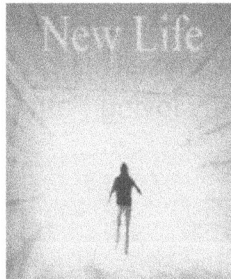

How To Praise God

Week 14 – Psalms 99: 3 - 4

Praise God For His Holiness, Mercy And Justice

*"Let them praise thy great and terrible name; [for] it [is] holy.
⁴The king's strength also loveth judgment thou dost establish
equity, thou executes judgment and righteousness in Jacob."*

What are you doing for God today? Are you complaining
about all that you have do? Did you stop to ask God how
He wants you to spend your day? Have you placed a
flower on your windowsill to remind you of the goodness
of Jesus? As you water and watch your flower blossom,
take a moment to praise God for His Holy power and for
allowing you to see another day.

Musical Selections:

Gospel: Your Grace and Mercy

Hymn: At Calvary

Prayer:

I am thanking you Lord for your mercies. I am thanking
you Lord, for your gratefulness. I am not going to wait for
the end of the week to get here before I stop and say
thank you. I am not going to wait until the pain and
sickness creep into my body, or wait until the pain and
sickness goes away. I am thanking you now Lord, for your
endless mercies and boundless love. Amen.

Week 15 – Ephesians 1:6

Praise God For His Grace

"To the praise of the glory of His grace, in which He has made us accepted in the One having been loved."

I love you, I love you, I love you Lord today. How many times during the week do you praise God for His love? The greatest gift of all is God's grace and salvation. God has given us eternal life and this life is in His Son, Jesus Christ. God has freely given us salvation in exchange for His own pleasure. He loves us even when we do not love ourselves. This is His agape love. His praise shall forever be in my heart.

Musical Selections:

> **Gospel:** Grace, Grace God's Awesome Grace

> **Hymn:** God's Amazing Grace

Prayer:

I love you Lord with all my heart. Thank you for the gift of life and wonderful miracles you have worked in my life. I give you praise for all the things you have allowed me to do. I lift your name which is above all names. All praises are forever yours. Amen.

Week 16 – Psalms 135: 3

Praise God For His Goodness

"Praise the LORD; for the LORD is good: sing praises unto his name; for it is pleasant."

The goodness of God is His outward manifestation of His will. The goodness of God covers all the works of His hands. God's goodness is displayed in His creation, in man's redemption, and in His providence.

God is originally good – Creatures may be good, but their goodness comes from and is granted to them by God.

God is infinitely good – His goodness is boundless and has no limits.

God is perfectly good – Nothing has an absolute perfect goodness but God.

God is immutably good – God's immutable goodness is from eternity to eternity.

Musical Selections:

> **Gospel:** God Is a Good God

> **Hymn**: O How I Love Jesus

Prayer:

Thank you, Lord, for choosing me. Thank you, Lord, for loving me. Thank you, Father. Amen.

Week 17 – Psalms 117

Praise God For His Kindness

"O praise the LORD, all ye nations: praise Him, all ye people. For His merciful kindness is great toward us: and the truth of the LORD endureth for ever. Praise Ye the LORD."

God cares for me and He cares for you. During times of meditation, you should ask God for His kindness to bestow you with His love. Stop what you are doing and give God this moment praising Him saying, I love the Lord because He heard my cry. Lord, you pitied all of my groans. Long as I live and as long as troubles rise, I know that I will hasten to your throne.

Musical Selections:

Gospel: I Am a Friend of God

Hymn: Praise Him

Prayer:

Lord, you are loving, amazing, kind, giving, patient, strong, good, encouraging, comforting, mighty, and inspiring. Thank you, Father, for your kindness. Amen.

Week 18 – Ephesians 2:8 – 9

Praise God For His Salvation

"For by grace are ye saved through faith; and that not of yourselves: it is the gift of God: [9]Not of works, lest any man should boast."

All believers are commanded to praise God! In fact, Isaiah 43:21 explains that praise is one reason we were created, "This people I have formed for Myself; they shall declare My praise." Hebrews 13:15 confirms this: "Through Jesus, therefore, let us continually offer to God a sacrifice of praise - the fruit of lips that confess His name."

Musical Selections:

Gospel: Hallelujah, Salvation and Glory

Hymn: Lead Me, Guide Me

Prayer:

Reveal yourself to me, Lord, in your word so that I may stand firmly on your foundation. I'll drop to my knees when I can no longer stand. And I will not stop praising your name. Amen.

Week 19 – Psalms 71

Praise God For The Hard Times

"You have allowed me to suffer much hardship, but you will restore me to life again and lift me up from the depths of the earth. You will restore me to even greater honor and comfort me once again. Then I will praise you with music on the harp, because you are faithful to your promises, O God. I will sing for you with a lyre, O Holy One of Israel. I will shout for joy and sing your praises, for you have redeemed me."

Sometimes there is so much drama in your life, you do not know if you are coming or going. You do not know if you should turn right, turn left or merely stand still. These are the times when you have to let go and let God have His way in your life. These are the times when you need to stop and listen to what God is telling you to do. God will not let you down, for He is omnipresent.

Musical Selections:

> **Gospel:** Abundantly Blessed

> **Hymn:** Guide Me, O Thou Great Jehovah

Prayer:

Thank you, Lord, for the amazing work of the Holy Spirit in my life. Amen.

Week 20 – Psalms 111:7 - 8

Praise God For His Great Works

"His handy-works are truth and right; all His commands are sure: And, done in truth and uprightness, they evermore endure."

God's Word is *eternal*. His word is firm and established. You give God praise for the wonderful, marvelous works that He has done for you. You exalt His name because He remembers the covenant He made with Abraham. You praise His name because He is Lord of Lords and King of Kings. His Word is unchanging and His word is sure. Oh praise for the great works He has done in your life.

Musical Selections:

Gospel: Jesus Can Work It Out

Hymn: May the Work I've Done, Speak for Me

Prayer:

I have been ceaselessly praying to you, Father, for all the things you have provided for me. I love you more and more everyday. Amen.

Week 21 – Psalms 150:1

Praise God For His Acts Of Power

"Praise Ye the Lord. Praise God in His sanctuary: praise Him in the firmament of His Power."

Power sometimes signifies authority, and a man is said to be mighty and powerful in regard of his dominion, and the right he has to command others, but authority and power must be kept distinct. The power of God is seen in those commissions in the air and earth: such as thunders, lightning storms, earthquakes and hurricanes. Consider the following:

1. God's power *in preservation*. No creature has power to preserve itself: see Psalms 36:6.

2. God's power *in government*. He even restrained the malice of Satan: see Psalms 93:3-4.

3. God's power *in judgment*. When He smites, none can resist Him: see Ezekiel 22:14.

God's power is self-existent and self-sustained. Therefore, call on Him in your time of need and praise Him, thereby fueling joy, which is your strength.

Musical Selections:

Gospel: Jesus Can Work It Out

Hymn: May the Work I've Done, Speak for Me

Prayer:

Faith is the substance of things hoped for, the evidence of things not seen. Lord, make me a channel of peace. Amen.

Week 22 – Psalms 150:2

Praise God For His Greatness

"Praise Him for His mighty acts: praise Him according to His excellent greatness."

God is great and He is worthy to be praised. I cannot help but move my shoulders and pat my feet when I hear the song, "I Love to Praise Him". I thank Him for waking me up each and every day and for allowing the faculties of my body to work as they should. Do you feel as happy as I do? Do you feel like jumping up and down, running down the aisle of the church, shouting from the rooftop: "God is great and He is worthy to be praised! He is my mighty fortress and my joy for tomorrow. He is my all and all. I will praise Him all day long. I will praise Him tomorrow and I will praise Him for His excellent greatness."

Musical Selections:

> **Gospel:** All Day Long, I've Been With Jesus

> **Hymn:** My Faith Looks Up To Thee

Prayer:

Lord, help me to keep everything in check and in perspective, including myself. Amen.

Week 23 – Psalms 17:3

Praise God For Who He Is

"Thou hast proved mine heart; thou hast visited me in the night; thou hast tried me, and shalt find nothing; I am purposed that my mouth shall not transgress."

The angels do not need hymn books: they just pour out the music as it fills their hearts. It is not like that with us on earth. We are limited here by our physical environment, even if we have good voices — which some of us don't have! The point is, we should have an inner bent of mind towards praise to God. Therefore, praise Him for His almighty power. This is the day the Lord has made, let us be glad and rejoice in it.

Musical Selections:

> **Gospel:** Let's Get Back to Eden

> **Hymn:** He Is Lord

Prayer:

Consecrate me to His praise and to the wholehearted love of all my brothers and sisters and order all my days and deeds in your peace. For You are my Life, my hope, my joy and my healing. My Eternal Father, I send You glory. Amen.

Week 24 – Psalms 135:6

Praise God For His Sovereignty

"Whatsoever the LORD pleased, that did He in heaven, and in earth, in the seas, and all deep places."

When you praise God for His Sovereignty, you are praising Him for His whole Being. You are praising Him for His limitless love. You are praising Him for His everlasting chain that binds you to Him. You are praising Him for His grace and His mercy. You are praising Him for making you an heir to His throne.

Musical Selections:

> **Gospel:** Acceptable To You

> **Hymn:** Look and Live

Prayer:

I praise you, Lord, for your Sovereignty. Amen.

Week 25 – Judges 5:3

Praise God For He Is My King

"Hear, O ye kings; give ear, O ye princes, I, even I, will sing unto the Lord; I will sing praise to the Lord God of Israel."

My Lord is my King and in Him will I trust. When things seem to be falling apart around you, do you still trust the Lord to bring you through your crisis or do you look to work things out yourself?

There is no fear in trust: the two are opposites. When we really fear, we are not fully trusting. When we trust, fear gives way to assurance.

Trust looks at things as they are. Trust sees the dangers that threaten, and assesses them at their true value. Trust sees the difficulties, and does not discount them. Believe in God and remember, trust looks beyond your limited sight and sees God.

Musical Selections:

> **Gospel:** I Heard The Voice of Jesus

> **Hymn:** My Faith Looks Up To Thee

Prayer:

Heavenly Father, guide me in your ways and keep me in your care. Amen.

Week 26 – Psalms 16:1

Praise God For All The Reasons He Is Him First In My Life

"Preserve me, O God: for in Thee do I put my trust."

Heavenly Father, I raise my hand to thee. I start my day with a prayer and I end my night thanking you for the glorious day you provided me. I put you first in my life and I seek your guidance every day. You are my mentor, my supreme leader. Each day I yield my life to you: to do your will, and to read and obey your Word.

Musical Selections

Gospel: Lead My Jesus, Lead Me

Hymn: Lead Me, Lord

Prayer

Lord, God, You are my provider, I praise You and I love You. Amen.

Praise God Because...

Week 27 – Revelation 1:8

Praise God Because He Is Alpha And Omega

"I am Alpha and Omega, the beginning and the ending, saith the Lord, which is, and which was, and which is to come, the Almighty."

In majesty of power, in dignity of grace, in beauty of virtue and in eternity of love, Christ is without compare. Who is qualified to write a preface to One who stands in priority to all truth, who is both source and substance of all truth? How can anyone write a history of the Creator, who preceded the calendars of time and who holds precedence over all men whom He created?

The Lord delights in our praise and worship. He longs to hear the sound of worship pouring forth from the heart, THROUGH the mouths of His children. As much as we long for Him and desire Him, He longs for us and desires our praise! Through praise we pour out our love, our gratitude, our adoration for Him. We praise Him simply for who He is, for His greatness, power and majesty. We praise Him because though we are undeserving of His blessings, His goodness, His mercy and grace, He still freely gives it while we are yet still sinners.

Musical Selections:

> **Gospel:** Alpha and Omega

> **Hymn:** The Greatest Of These Is Love

Prayer:

O Lord, you know how busy I must be this day.
If I forget you, please do not forget me. Amen.

Week 28 – 2 Samuel 6:5

Praise God Because He Is Real

"And David and all the house of Israel played before the Lord on all manner of instruments made of fir wood, even on harps, and on psalteries, and on timbrels, and on comets and on cymbals."

God has authorized and scripture supports the use of musical instruments in song. Do not hesitate to praise God with your heart, soul and mind. Sometimes the best praise you can give God is when you are singing alone in the shower. That is when you are washing away your troubles, cleansing and removing the dirt and grime from your body. As the penetrating beads of warm water stream down your body, you feel as if you can reach out and touch God. You can feel God taking control of your life. It is at that moment that you know God is real. He is real! Yes, He is real in your soul.

Musical Selections:

Gospel: Real, Real, Jesus Is Real to Me

Hymn: Yes God Is Real

Prayer:

Lord, I praise you in good times and I praise you in bad times. I praise you when I am happy and I praise when I am sad. You are my light and my fortress; in You I need no other. I lift my hands to give you praise. I lift my hands to you, Father, and I sing praises unto you. Amen.

Week 29 – Jeremiah 17:14

Praise God Because He Saves

"Heal me, O Lord, and I shall be healed; save me, and I shall be saved: for thou art my Praise."

Praise God when you get up in the morning. Praise God when you go to bed at night. Praise God before you start your day. Praise God when you finish your day, thanking Him for keeping you safe along the way.

Musical Selections:

Gospel: Blessed

Hymn: He Touched Me

Prayer:

Lord, you were there for me, when I did not know how to get myself out of a bad situation. You were there for me, when I thought that I had walked my last mile. You were there for me, when I had no one to turn to. You were there for me and saved my soul. Oh Father, I will praise your name forevermore. Amen.

Week 30 – Psalms 8:2

Praise God Because He Paralyzes The Enemy

"When you praise God, you paralyze the enemy."

Once you are in the habit of praying, prayers of praise will become spontaneous. Prayer will allow you to spend more devotional time studying the scriptures. Prayer will weaken the enemy and build your courage to step out on faith and trust Him more each day. When you know that, your enemy is paralyzed and cannot harm you, it is then time for you to get your praise on.

Musical Selections:

>   **Gospel:** I Love You Lord

>   **Hymn:** Great is Thy Faithfulness

Prayer:

Thank you, Lord, for the multiple promises I have received from you. Amen.

Week 31 – 1 Chronicles 16:25

Praise God Because He Is Worthy To Be Praised

"For great is the LORD, and greatly to be praised: he also is to be feared above all gods."

Hallelujah, for You are worthy to be praised. I love you for your grace and mercy. I praise you because of your gift of salvation. You sent your Son Jesus to die for my sins so that I might live again. They placed a crown of thorns on His head, they drove nails in His hands, they drove nails in His feet and they pierced His sides. Yet Jesus still loves me.

I may forget to praise you, God. Yet you still love me. I may forget to thank you for my glorious day. Yet you still love me. I may forget to ask you to protect me. Yet you still love me. I may forget to bless my food. Yet you still love me.

Musical Selections:

Gospel: Worthy Is The Lamb

Hymn: More About Jesus

Prayer:

God of our Fathers, You are worthy to be praised. You are worthy of all the glory for you are omnipotent and holy. Amen.

Week 32 – Isaiah 42:10

Praise God Because My Mouth Will Speak His Praise

"Sing unto the Lord; a new song, and His praise from the end of the earth; ye that go down to the sea, and all that is therein; the isles, and the inhabitants thereof."

Is it not mind-boggling how some people you know will celebrate with you in private, but ignore you in public? They benefit from your gifts but fail to give you recognition for what they have received. Has that ever happened to you? What about this: You see she acts like she does not even know you. This is not a good feeling. Scenes like this may happen because the person who did not speak to you may be ashamed, scared, angry, embarrassed or afraid to disclose to her friends that she knows you.

How many times have you forgotten to acknowledge God? One, two, three, six, thirty, everyday? Peter denied Jesus three times. He was afraid to acknowledge that he was associated with Jesus. Now is your time to do an about face and try praising your Lord and Savior. We are all in a relationship with God every day and He deserves our praise.

Musical Selections:

> **Gospel:** I Go To the Rock

> **Hymn:** Crown Him With Many Crowns

Prayer:

Without you Father, I am nothing. Keep me in your tender loving care. Amen.

Week 33 – Jeremiah 20:13

Praise God Because He Saves Me From The Hands Of The Evildoers

"Sing unto the Lord, praise ye the Lord: for he hath delivered the soul of the poor from the hand of evildoers."

Did you ever wonder why you were the only one standing after the dust clears? Did you brag that it was your clever thinking and your amazing wit? Did you start to analyze and strategize your next move? Stop! You know better. It was not you, but God who delivered you from your evildoers. It was God who stopped to think of little old you and have mercy on you. It was God who brought you out. Go out and spread the word through your praise. Shout from the rooftop the praise of how He delivered you. Shout from the mountaintop the goodness of God. He is your deliverer and your protector, keeping you from the harm of evildoers.

Musical Selections:

Gospel: Lord, It Was You Who Brought Me Out

Hymn: We Bring A Sacrifice of Praise

Prayer:

O Lord, How Excellent Is Your Name. Amen.

Week 34 – Psalms 107:9

Praise God Because Of His Benefits

"For he satisfieth the longing soul, and filleth the hungry soul with goodness."

God fed the multitude on the bank of the river. They gathered to listen to His teachings. Today, we must read His Word, seek and find understanding of how to be a child of the King. Reading biblical materials helps us fill and feed our spiritual soul.

How does praise affect the believer? When we praise God, we are acknowledging that it is not our own efforts that produce blessings and prosperity. In Deuteronomy, chapters 7 and 8, the children of Israel are told to remember to thank God for the abundance they will receive. It was God, not their own efforts, which gave them wealth. The more we praise God, the more humble we become. Haven't you heard the good news? Praise makes us humble.

Musical Selections:

    Gospel: I Want To Go Where Jesus Is

    Hymn: Jesus Saves

Prayer:

Help me, Father, to overcome temptations during my day. As I read and study your Word, I will grow stronger to fight off the enemy. I will love, honor and praise your name forevermore. Amen.

Week 35 – Psalms 66:8

Praise God Because He Demands To Be Heard

"O bless our God, ye people, and make the voice of his praise to be heard."

It is obvious that God wants our praise. Throughout the Bible, God explains to us how we should praise Him. Our Praise should not be silent but with great noise. We should shout it loudly to the mountaintops, "Great is God and He is worthy to be praised". Psalms 119:64 states "Seven times a day I will praise you for your righteous judgments." There are over 243 usages of praise in the Old and New Testament, depending on which version of the Bible you are using. Start your "**Praise Diet**" right now and renew your faith in the Lord.

Musical Selections:

>   **Gospel:** All Because of Jesus

>   **Hymn:** This Is the Day That the Lord Hath Made

Prayer:

Remember who I am, Lord: I am your child. Mold me and make me in your image. Guide me along the way as I experiment with my praise to You. Holy, holy! Worthy, worthy! You alone are to be lifted up on high, worshipped and glorified. My King, You are beautiful in all Your ways, pure and righteous, above all others. You are the Lamb of God and I choose to worship you. You loved me first without reservation, even to the sacrifice on the cross at Calvary. You reach out from heaven to this earth and willingly draw me to Yourself. You provide all my needs, and You charge me to trust in You and live a life of peace. Amen.

Week 36 – Psalms 22:3

Praise God Because He Inhabits The Praises Of His People

"But thou art holy, O thou that inhabitest the praises of Israel."

Perhaps you have heard your Worship Leader in your church proclaim that God inhabits the praises of His people. This is one of God's principle works. This means that praising God brings you to His presence and power. What better way to illustrate this truth than through the story of Paul and Silas in Acts 16.

Both were arrested, severely beaten and imprisoned. One might think praying and praising God would have been the last thing Paul and Silas would have considered doing. But that was exactly what they did! Suddenly, there was an earthquake. The prison doors swung wide open and Paul, Silas and all the other prisoners were released from their bondage. Their **praises** unleashed the mighty power of God.

Musical Selections:

> **Gospel:** Lift Your Head

> **Hymn:** Praise Him

Prayer:

I will always praise You for who You are and what You have done for me in my life. Amen.

Week 37 – Psalms 106:1

Praise God Because He Is Love

"Praise ye the LORD. O give thanks unto the LORD; for he is good: for his mercy endureth for ever."

How I love thee! Let me count the ways. Praise is not a fad and praise is not a charismatic theme. In 1 Chronicles 23:5, King David was so convinced of the power of praise he went out and employed over 4,000 people to perform it.

Praise is an essential part of keeping filled with the power and Spirit of our Lord and Savior. Why do you give God praise? I give praise to God because He first loved me. The Lord's Prayer begins and ends with praise. I praise God for how loving He is. Jesus rescued me from the dominion of darkness and brought me into the kingdom of the Son He loves. That is worth praising. Come on and get your praise on. I end each prayer with the word Amen, because it means "to be loyal", "to be certain", and "to place faith in". I place my faith in God, you should do the same.

Musical Selections:

> **Gospel:** We Adore Thee

> **Hymn:** My Faith Looks Up To Thee

Prayer:

I pray that I will always have a song and praise in my heart. Amen.

Week 38 – Isaiah 12:1

Praise God Because Even In Anger He Comforts Me

"And in that day thou shalt say, O LORD, I will praise thee: though thou wast angry with me, thine anger is turned away, and thou comfortedst me."

Praise God from whom all blessings flow!. He was angry with me, but now He comforts me. Oh, how the Holy Father comforts me. My God has come to save me. I will trust Him and not be afraid. My God has come to save me. He is my strength and He is my song. I will drink from the fountain, where salvation springs. I will shout for joy, for He is my strength and my song.

Musical Selections:

> **Gospel:** My God Has Come to Save Me

> **Hymn:** The Name of Jesus

Prayer:

I pray that I may at all times keep my mind open to new ideas.

I pray that I may learn the peace that comes with forgiving and the strength I gain in loving; that I may learn to take nothing for granted in this life; that I may learn to see and understand with my heart; that I may learn to humble myself in time of pain. Amen.

Week 39 – Joel 2:26

Praise God Because He Protects Us

"And ye shall eat in plenty, and be satisfied, and praise the name of the Lord your God, that hath dealt wondrously with you: and my people shall never be ashamed."

Our protection is in His power and in His name (John 17:12). This is an interesting comment on the relationship between Jesus and the Apostles. He protected them. The source of His power is in His name. His name stands for all the power and authority of the Godhead. His presence and power kept the Apostles safe and from harm. But now Jesus was approaching His time to leave; their relationship was about to change. Therefore, Jesus moves from praise to petition; from their past security, to their future sanctification.

The praise and power of God are made visible when…
- *We continue to follow Christ in the face of great trouble*
- *We believe the gospel and are changed by it*
- *We proclaim our ministry in Jesus Christ*
- *We affirm openly our love for one another*

Musical Selections:

Gospel: Glad I've Got Jesus

Hymn: Praise God From Whom All Blessing Flow

Prayer:

Lord, give me courage to speak with truth. Help me to extend the gentle hand of mercy and forgiveness to those who do not reverence your gift of grace and salvation. Amen.

New Testament Praise

Midnight Praise With Paul And Silas
Acts 16:25 – 34 (ESV)

About midnight Paul and Silas were praying and singing hymns to God, and the prisoners were listening to them, and suddenly there was a great earthquake, so that the foundations of the prison were shaken. And immediately all the doors were opened, and everyone's bonds were unfastened. When the jailer woke and saw that the prison doors were open, he drew his sword and was about to kill himself, supposing that the prisoners had escaped. But Paul cried with a loud voice, "Do not harm yourself, for we are all here." And the jailer called for lights and rushed in, and trembling with fear he fell down before Paul and Silas.

Then he brought them out and said, "Sirs, what must I do to be saved?" And they said, "Believe in the Lord Jesus, and you will be saved, you and your household." And they spoke the word of the Lord to him and to all who were in his house.

And he took them the same hour of the night and washed their wounds; and he was baptized at once, he and all his family. Then he brought them up into his house and set food before them. And he rejoiced along with his entire household that he had believed in God.

"I"

Week 40 – Matthew 21:16

I Will Perfect My Praise To You

"And said unto him, Hearest thou what these say? And Jesus saith unto them, Yea; have ye never read, Out of the mouth of babes and sucklings thou hast perfected praise?"

What should you do to perfect your praise with God? You must spend time reading God's word. You must spend time walking and talking with God to perfect your praise. You must read God's Word more than sitting around watching your favorite television show.

To start your **"Praise Diet"**, pick up your Bible and spend time in the Book of Psalms, which will help you to expand your praise vocabulary. Do not let the very tongue you use to praise God become the same tongue you use to gossip and slander your fellow church members. Use your words carefully. Speak them like your dying thoughts. Reverence God in His Holiness and praise Him forevermore.

Musical Selections:

>**Gospel:** Perfect Praise

>**Hymn:** Every Day With Jesus

Prayer:

May the words of my mouth and the meditations of my heart be pleasing in your sight, O Lord, my rock and my Redeemer. Amen.

Week 41 – Luke 18:43

I Will Praise God While I Have A Chance

"And immediately he received his sight, and followed him, glorifying God: and all the people, when they saw it, gave praise unto God."

When God works miracles in your life, do you plan to spend the rest of your life serving Him? Did you find the answer to your burning question? Was God almighty in the midst of your answer? Have you thanked God for being so good to you? Did you thank Him for waking you up this morning and starting you on your way? Has He been good to you lately? Do you feel the urge to shout around the house and shout out to the world how much you love Him? Oh yes, God is good, He has carried you through this treacherous life. When you could not see your way through, He was there for you. When you were down to your last dime, He made a way for you. When you said, "No way," God said, "Yes, you can." When you fell down on your knees in pain, crying, heartbroken, perplexed and bewildered, God helped you up and started you running again. Yes, you should praise Him while you have a chance.

Musical Selections:

> **Gospel:** For The Rest of My Life, I'll Serve Him

> **Hymn:** Blessed Be the Name

Prayer:

Hear my prayer, O Lord: hear my prayer, O Lord. Incline Thine ear to me and grant me thy peace. Amen.

Week 42 – John 9:24

I Have Sinned And Fallen Short Of God's Grace, Yet I Still Praise The Lord

"Then again called they the man that was blind, and said unto him, Give God the praise: we know that this man is a sinner."

Yes, I have sinned because I was born into sin. We all have sinned and fallen short of God's grace. Even after I sinned, God stepped down and picked me up out of the mire of my despair. Beyond any measures of my own, beyond any omissions of my own, God still loves me and He still bestows me with His grace. He loves me when I do right and loves me when I do wrong. He loves me in spite of myself. I know that His yoke is easy and His burden is light. I've found it so; yes, I have found it so. His service is my sweetest delight and His blessings ever flow.

Therefore, I will praise my God, who has given this minute, this hour, this day in my life. I will forever love Him who keeps the blood flowing warm in my body because He heard my cry and pitied my soul. Long as I live; yes, as long as I live, I will praise the Holy name of Jesus, Jesus, Jesus!

Musical Selections:

    Gospel: Yet Praise Him

    Hymn: His Yoke Is Easy

Prayer:

I thank God for His saving grace and I will praise His name through it all. Amen.

Week 43 – Romans 15:11

I Will Praise Him In The Midst Of Friends

"And again, Praise the Lord, all ye Gentiles; and laud him, all ye people."

Have you ever shared your spiritual experience with your friends telling them how God has truly blessed you? Were you overcome with joy and you felt like praising God all day? When I am overcome with joy, I want everyone to know it and I call my friends to tell them the good news.

God wants us to share the good news about His grace. He expects us to tell of His redeeming power and how He brought His Son to earth to save us from our sins. So go out into your community and praise the Lord. Praise God in the morning, praise God in the noonday, praise God in the evening and praise God in the midnight hour. Always praise the Lord.

Musical Selections:

> **Gospel:** We Must Praise

> **Hymn:** When the Praises Go Up, The Blessing Come Down

Prayer:

Heavenly Father, I come to You now in the name of my Lord and Savior Jesus Christ. Amen.

Week 44 – Ephesians 1:12

I Will Praise Him Regardless

"That we should be to the praise of His glory, who first trusted in Christ."

Because I trust in the Lord, I will praise His name forevermore. We have many reasons for loving the Lord, such as in times of joy and happiness, in times of distress, in times of sickness and in times of pain. Many times we forget to praise God during the adversities in our lives because we think God has deserted us. When we refuse to praise God in the midst of adversity, we accept the fate of our enemy. God has not deserted us; he is teaching and training us how to become stronger in His word. We must always obey and trust in the Lord. In Psalms 34:1, the psalmist states, "I will bless the Lord at all times and His praise shall continually be in my mouth." There is one thing I know about King David: he was all about praising the Lord, even though he had many shortcomings and many faults of his own. Remember, praise is your spiritual weapon against the enemy.

Musical Selections:

    Gospel: Praise Him In Advance

    Hymn: All Things Come of Thee

Prayer:

Dear Lord, give me the strength to obey thy commandments and to always remember to read your Word. Amen.

Week 45 – Philippians 1:11

I Will Praise God Today

"Being filled with the fruits of righteousness, which are by Jesus Christ, unto the glory and praise of God."

The New Testament joins praise and glory together. The glory of the Lord is not found in a holy mountain or in Jerusalem (the temple). But the glory of the Lord is found in those of us who abide in Jesus Christ in Spirit and in Truth. Believe it or not, this is where true worship takes place. This is where we have the ability to praise God. The glory which we often seek externally is always within us. The glory is our fruits of righteousness: love, joy, peace, patience and longsuffering. When we worship God, we should also praise Him.

Musical Selections:

> **Gospel:** The Glory of The Lord

> **Hymn:** Glory To His Name

Prayer:

Lord, how beautiful and holy is Your name. I will take whatever draws me closer to You. You give so that I can give it right back to You, as You so graciously did for David in 1 Chronicles 29:14. In my life, in my time, on this earth, it is not my will, but thine and thine alone. Amen

Week 46 Acts 2:47

I Am In His Favor, That Is Why I Praise Him

"Praising God, and having favour with all the people. And the Lord added to the church daily such as should be saved."

I am in God's favor because He has blessed me and He has blessed my family. I fall down on my knees and thank Him for the wondrous and profound love I get from my Heavenly Father. I am in His favor and part of His promise.

I grow in favor with the Lord as I faithfully live for the Lord. Psalms 30:5 tells me that when I continually draw closer to the Lord, I can dwell in His favor.

Musical Selections:

> **Gospel:** It Is A Good Thing to Give Thanks Unto the Lord

> **Hymn:** He's Sweet I Know

Prayer:

Father, I want to be in your favor. I thank you for all of the blessings you have given me especially those that I failed to recognize. Thank you for loving me unconditionally. Thank you for always providing for me. Thank you even more for the work you have been doing in my life. Thank you for all of the lessons I have learned and for lessons I have yet to learn from your teachings. Father, I thank you for your endless grace and mercy. Please forgive my sins and moments or years of weakness. I am so sorry for the times I failed to praise your name or acknowledge you as my Lord and Savior. Father, I love you with my whole heart. Amen.

Week 47 – Philippians 4:8

I Have Received A Good Report, Now I Am Getting My Praise On

"Finally, brethren, whatsoever things are true, whatsoever things are honest, whatsoever things are just, whatsoever things are pure, whatsoever things are lovely, whatsoever things are of good report; if there be any virtue, and if there be any praise, think on these things."

Father, if there be any praise in me I will praise Your name. Take those newspaper headlines you are reading and take them to the altar. Take your medical report, your credit rating, your child's report card, and the pictures of your loved ones; spread them out before the Lord as a way of entrusting them to Him. The Bible states, "Cast your burdens on the Lord and He will support you." God will never allow the righteous to be forsaken.

In Isaiah 37:16-20, Hezekiah prayed, "Lord of hosts, God of Israel, who is enthroned above all cherubim, You are God, You alone, of all the kingdoms of the earth..." Hezekiah's prayer is one of the most effective prayers in Scripture, resulting in creating the most powerful army the world has ever seen. Hezekiah received a good report from the Lord.

Musical Selections:

> **Gospel:** Praise Him In the Storm

> **Hymn:** Are Ye Able Said The Master

Prayer:

Father, I thank you that the storm was not as bad as it could have been. Amen.

Week 48 – Hebrews 2:12

I Believe In Fellowship And Praise

"Saying, I will declare thy name unto my brethren, in the midst of the church will I sing praise unto thee."

Believe it, proclaim it and rejoice in it for you shall be made whole. Stand still and know that I am God Almighty. Stand up and declare the power of God; stand up and proclaim that He is Lord of Lords and He alone will protect you and care for you. Lift up the name of Jesus in the midst of your song. Declare His almighty righteousness and believe it.

Know that Jesus is Lord of His day, He is Master of His own day, which is the Lord's Day (Rev1:10). To be sure that you have fellowship with Jesus, you must know Him for yourself. For you to remain in fellowship with Jesus, you must keep His teachings. As long as you abide in Jesus, there is a union or an attachment. From this union or attachment comes a communion or a sharing, and with sharing comes praise and fellowship. You do not want to lose your fellowship with your Lord and Savior.

Musical Selections:

Gospel: Lord I Believe You

Hymn: I Will Trust In the Lord

Prayer:

Dear God, anoint me to follow Thy will. Amen.

Week 49 – Hebrews 13:15

I Will Praise Him Because Of His Sacrifice

"By him therefore let us offer the sacrifice of praise to God continually, that is, the fruit of our lips giving thanks to his name."

I am going to keep on holding on to His hand. I am going to keep my hand in the hand of the Author of the greatest book ever written. Every time I keep God's plan first and foremost in my life, my needs are not only met, but are surpassed and surpassed in more ways than I could ever imagine. I love you, Lord, because of your sacrifice. I know that my God is able to do what He said He would do. I will offer up the sacrifice of praise.

Musical Selections:

> **Gospel:** I Won't Let Go Of His Hand

> **Hymn:** Are You Able Said The Master

Prayer:

Lord, You are the God who made the heavens and the earth. I praise You with all my heart for Your loving care. Amen.

Week 50 – 1 Peter 1:7

I Have A Praise In My Heart

"That the trial of your faith, being much more precious than of gold that perisheth, though it be tried with fire, might be found unto praise and honour and glory at the appearing of Jesus Christ."

What we praise indicates our mindset. I praise God when I am driving; I praise God when I am down so that I can feel better. Have you ever noticed that people whose hearts are filled with praise have a serene peaceful beauty about them. They do not seem to be tormented. People who cannot praise appear to become sour, grumpy and anxious. It is in their body language; they have poisoned themselves and have become very toxic to themselves and to the people around them.

If you feel that you are in a drowning situation, try the **PRAISE DIET** for 30 consecutive days. You will see a change in your life; your friends and loved ones will notice the change in you. You should remember God does not need our praise, but God knows that we need it and that is why He rejoices in it. God knows that without praise we will feel inadequate, ugly, miserable and sad.

Musical Selections:

    Gospel: When You Praise

    Hymn: The Hallelujah Chorus

Prayer:

There is healing for my soul, Lord. Please help me find it. Amen.

Week 51 – 1 Peter 4:11

I Will Praise God When I Start A Conversation With My Neighbor

"If any man speak, let him speak as the oracles of God; if any man minister, let him do it as of the ability which God giveth: that God in all things may be glorified through Jesus Christ, to whom be praise and dominion for ever and ever."

Television show host Joan Rivers opened up her show with this slogan "Can We Talk?" Lord, I fail to talk about You when I should. I know that I need to communicate with You more than I do. I know that I do not know You as well as I should. I have heard about You and I have read about You in many books. I am grateful for all that You have done for me. You sent Your son Jesus to earth to show me how to love my neighbors.

Thank you, Father, for Your love and mercy.

Musical Selections:

> **Gospel:** How Great Is Our God

> **Hymn:** Under His Wings

Prayer:

Lord, I believe in the power of prayer for I am your faithful and humble servant. Amen.

Week 52 – Revelations 19:5

I Will Praise God for the Small and Great Things in My Life

"And a voice came out of the throne, saying, Praise our God, all ye his servants, and ye that fear him, both small and great."

God has such a strong presence in my life. He has carried me through some tough times and the real lows in my life. He carried me when I could not even see the sunshine for the forest. Do you know what? Even in my times of distress and sorrow I praise Him for waking me up each morning and giving me the ability to see my loved ones. I praise Him for giving me the ability to drink a glass of fresh cold water or sip a cup of hot brewed coffee. I praise Him for giving me the ability to hug and kiss my loved ones and tell them how much I love them. I praise Him for the ability to hear my parents' voices on the other end of the phone. I praise Him for the ability to smell fresh cut grass or to smell the aromas of a holiday dinner simmering in the kitchen. I praise God for my five senses and that I am all wrapped up in His Grace. God has been and continues to be good to me and I know God has been good to you. I will praise Him for all of the small and great things He has done in my life. As long as I have breath in my body, I will praise His name forever.

Musical Selections:

> **Gospel:** Total Praise

> **Hymn:** I Heard The Voice of Jesus Say

Prayer: Lord, Lord, Lord you have been so good to me. Let me not forget the presence and power of your love because you are Alpha and Omega. Amen.

BONUS:

GET ON THE 30-DAY PRAISE DIET PLAN

BONUS

GET ON THE 30-DAY PRAISE DIET PLAN

The next page begins the **30-Day Praise Diet Plan** to help you strengthen your walk with God.

This is a proven plan of Praise! At the end of this plan you will have a better outlook on life. You will experience God working in your life. When you do, you will want to share your praise with others. Tell your friends and family how God has blessed you. But most of all you need to get up and get your praise on!

How to Use the 30-Day Praise Diet Plan

Each day provides you with:
- A special characteristic of God
- How you should focus on His greatness--
  - Who He is and what He is to you.

For the months that have 31 days, there is one extra day of the plan.

Meditate on each scripture, give God your praise and do not forget to pray.

As you renew your strength in God, you will begin to notice that you are developing a daily devotion that is helpful in your efforts in praising God.

Take time now to Praise the Lord.

30-DAY PRAISE DIET PLAN

DAY 1: A PATIENT GOD (2 PETER 3:9)
I give you praise, Lord, because You are not negligent in your promise to me. Thank you for being patient with me.

DAY 2: THE GREATNESS OF GOD (JOB 36:26)
I give you praise, Lord, because as I learn more about your greatness, the greater you become in my life.

DAY 3: THE DELIVERER GOD (PSALMS 68:20)
I give you praise, Lord, for being my deliverance and my salvation, and for setting me free from sin.

DAY 4: THE GIVING GOD (JOHN 3:16)
I give you praise, Lord, for being a generous God, who did not stop short of giving your Son Jesus, who died on the cross for our sins.

DAY 5: THE ALMIGHTY GOD (PSALMS 89:8)
I give you praise, Lord, for You are mighty and your faithfulness surrounds me.

DAY 6: THE GOD OF GLORY (ISAIAH 22:24)
I give you praise, Lord, because everything you made, you said it was good. The heavens declared the glory of God, the skies proclaimed the works of his hands. God's very work praises Him and give brings Him glory.

DAY 7: THE CREATOR GOD (NEHEMIAH 9:6)
I give you praise, Lord, for You made the heavens, the starry hosts, the earth and all its glory, the seas and all that is within them. You give life to everything with the sound of your voice. It is done; it has happened.

DAY 8: THE EVERLASTING GOD (ISAIAH 9:6)

I give you praise, Lord; You live forever in my heart. Your everlasting love covers me and You live forever and ever.

DAY 9: THE ONLY GOD (ISAIAH 45:5)

I give you praise, Lord, because of who You are, and there is no other. You are Alpha and Omega. You are the beginning and the end.

DAY 10: THE HEALING GOD (EXODUS 15:26)

I give you praise, Lord, for You are the Lord who heals me.

DAY 11: THE BURDEN BEARER GOD (PSALMS 68:19)

I give you praise, Lord, for You bear all of my burdens. It is your footsteps that I see in the sand.

DAY 12: THE GOD WHO ANSWERS PRAYER (ISAIAH 65:24)

I give you praise, Lord, because You are a God who loves to answer prayer and who begins to answer my prayer even before I start praying.

DAY 13: THE MERCIFUL GOD (NEHEMIAH 9:31)

I give you praise, Lord, because You never forsake me. You are a merciful and a gracious God.

DAY 14: THE WISE GOD (JUDE 25)

I give you praise, Lord, for being the only God that can save me.

DAY 15: THE LIFTER OF MY HEAD GOD (PSALMS 3:3)

I give you praise, Lord, for You are a shield around me. O, Lord bestow your glory on me and lift up my head when I am weary, tired or sad.

DAY 16: THE GRACE OF GOD (ROMANS 5:21)
I give you praise, Lord, because of your grace. I have been set free. Your grace is an unmerited favor and is a true gift.

DAY 17: THE FORTRESS AND REFUGE GOD (PSALMS 62: 6-7)
I give you praise, Lord, because You are my rock and salvation. You are my fortress and refuge. My refuge is in You!

DAY 18: THE GOD OF ALL THE EARTH (ISAIAH 54:5)
I give you praise, Lord, because You are the Holy one. You are the God of all the earth.

DAY 19: THE COMPASSIONATE GOD (2 CORITHIANS 1:3)
I give you praise, Lord, because of your compassion and you are the God of all my comfort.

DAY 20: THE GOOD SHEPHERD (PSALMS 23:1)
I give you praise, Lord, because You shepherd me and guide me in the path of righteousness for Your name's sake.

DAY 21: THE LOVING GOD (1 JOHN 4:16)
I praise you, Lord, because you are a loving God.

DAY 22: THE GOD OF JOY (ROMANS 3:26)
I give you praise, Lord, for being a just God and for being my justifier. I believe in You and because of You will I receive joy.

DAY 23: THE GOD OF LIGHT (PSALMS 27:1)
I give you praise, Lord, because You are my light and my salvation. Whom then shall I fear?

DAY 24: THE GOD OF PEACE (ROMANS 16:20)
I give you praise, Lord, because You are the God of my peace. You are the reason for my calm. I have placed no other God before you.

DAY 25: THE GREAT LIBERATOR (PSALMS 70:5)
I give you praise, Lord, because You are my help and You liberate me from the evils of the earth.

DAY 26: THE MIRACLE WORKING GOD (PSALMS 77:14)
I give you praise, Lord, because You are the God who works miracles in my life. You are the God who displays your power to all mankind.

DAY 27: THE FAITHFUL GOD (LAMENTATIONS 3:23)
I give you praise, Lord, because of your great and abundant stability and faithfulness in my life. Every day You provide me something new.

DAY 28: THE FORGIVING GOD (NEHEMIAH 9:17)
I give you praise, Lord, because of your abounding love.

DAY 29: THE VICTORIOUS GOD (2 CORITHIANS 2:14)
I give you praise, Lord, because You protect me. My victorious God, it is You who leads me triumphantly towards the path of your praise.

DAY 30: THE HOLY GOD (REVELATION 4:8)
I give you praise, Lord, because You are holy. You are God almighty, who was, and who is and who is to come.

DAY 31: THE ETERNAL GOD (ISAIAH 57:15)
I give you praise, Lord, because your covenant with Abraham is everlasting and your blessings are endless and will last throughout eternity.

JOIN THE "PRAISE DIET'S" MAILING LIST
JOIN "ALL THE PRAISE" FAN CLUB AT

HTTP://WWW.FACEBOOK.COM

NAME:

_____

LAST   FIRST

STREET ADDRESS:

_____

CITY/STATE/ZIP:

_____

EMAIL ADDRESS:

_____

SEND INFORMATION REQUESTS TO:
OPHELIA@PRAISEDIET.COM or mail to
1923 Bragg St, #119, Sanford, NC 27330.

To schedule a workshop, purchase additional materials or request more information go to the website at:

http://www.praisediet.com

To order bulk supplies for your group
http://createspace/com/3401076

CALL TODAY: 1-866-579-7475

Triple J Publishing